Jazzin' Americana

1

9 Late Elementary Piano Solos That Celebrate American Jazz

Wynn-Anne Rossi

Welcome to *Jazzin' Americana*. This unique series is a personal journey through the jazz genre, honoring the history, diverse styles, and fabulous musicians who made this music great. While delving into appealing jazz styles, the performer will become familiar with the names of famous musicians like Louis Armstrong, Charlie Parker, and Miles Davis. From blues and bebop to boogie and rock, American jazz has made its profound mark on the music of the world.

Each piece is enhanced by interesting facts to awaken curiosity and broaden music education. Please encourage additional jazz listening and research as students navigate through the different styles. Rhythm workshops are included to help students count, then "feel" tricky jazz rhythms.

Please note that improvisation is not the focus of this series. Though improvisation is a key element in jazz, these books are designed as an introduction to the sounds of jazz. However, teachers and students may find it energizing to use a certain jazz style, left-hand pattern, or chord sequence as a springboard for free experimentation.

Enjoy this heartfelt, historic journey through *Jazzin' Americana*!

Wynn-Anne Rossi

Contents

Alfred Music
P.O. Box 10003
Van Nuys, CA 91410-0003
alfred.com

D1367221

ISBN-10: 1-4706-3680-8
ISBN-13: 978-1-4706-3680-7
Cover Illustration
Instrument Icons: © gettyimages.com / Leontura

Super Stomp Rag

Ragtime was a predecessor to early jazz. Composers like pianist Scott Joplin helped set the scene with playful, syncopated melodies. These melodies, combined with a march-like beat in the left hand, created a "ragged" rhythm and gave birth to the genre's name.

Rhythm Workshop

Tap rhythm 3x daily.

Mm. 6–8

Wynn-Anne Rossi

The audience may participate by lightly stomping one foot on beat 4.
Note: Audience stomps do not always coincide with performer stomps!

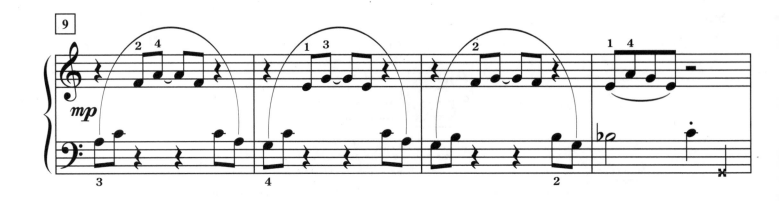

4

For Diane Majeski, who was there with me from the beginning!

In the Hall of the Jazz Kings*

"Preservation Hall. Now that's where you'll find all of the greats." —Louis Armstrong, trumpeter. This famous site features daily concerts of traditional jazz in the French Quarter of New Orleans.

Rhythm Workshop

Tap rhythm 3x daily.

Mm. 1–2

Wynn-Anne Rossi

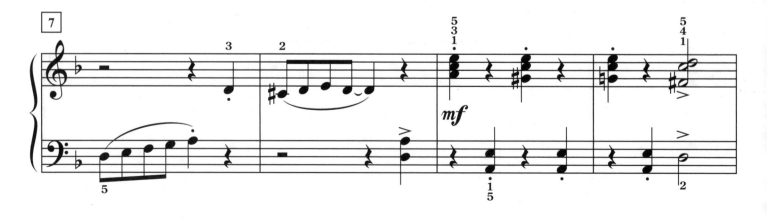

* Inspired by "In the Hall of the Mountain King" from Peer Gynt Suite No. 1, Op. 46 by Edvard Grieg

Practice the Piano Blues

The blues emerged from the African-American slave culture and the many hardships of life. Preceding jazz, it often included swing rhythm, the blues scale, and a 12-bar pattern of harmony.

Wynn-Anne Rossi

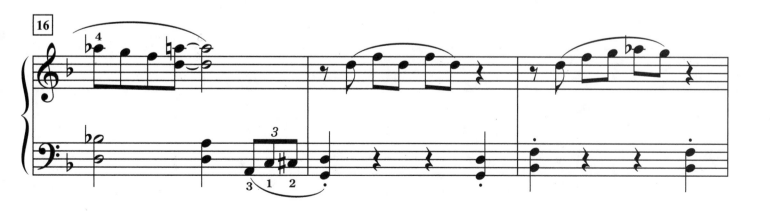

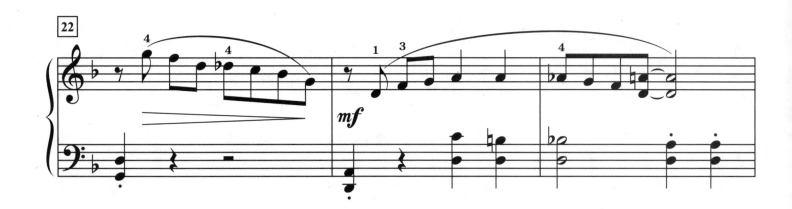

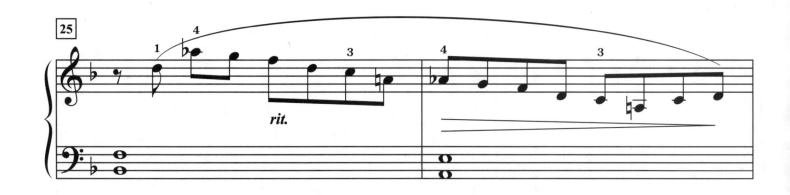

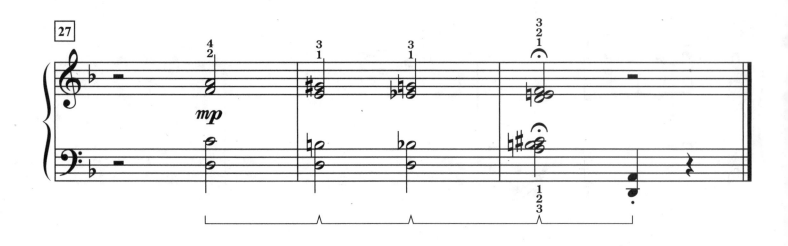

Woogie Boogie

Popular from the late 1920s into the 1950s, boogie woogie inspired people to dance! An ongoing, repeating bass line provides the driving rhythm that energizes the music.

Rhythm Workshop

Tap rhythm 3x daily.

Mm. 25–26

Wynn-Anne Rossi

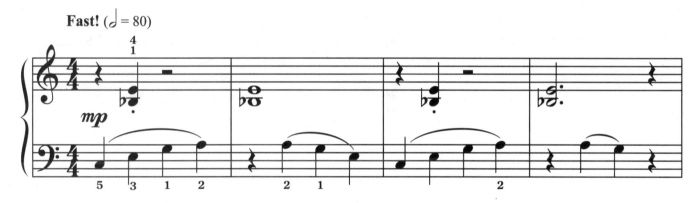

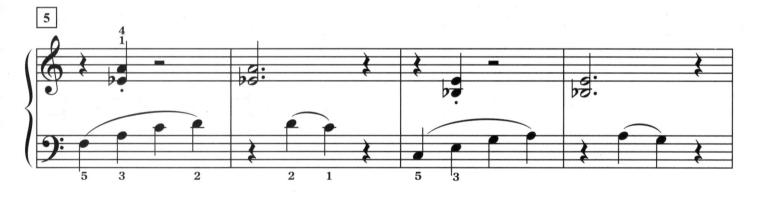

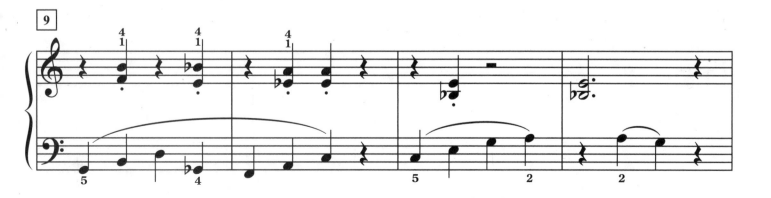

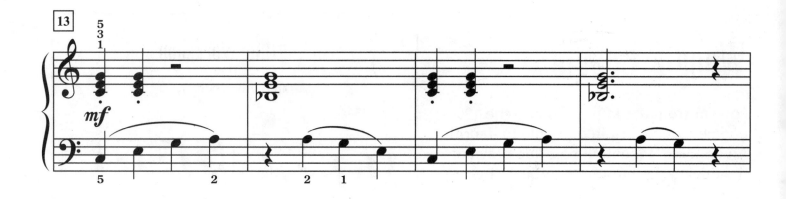

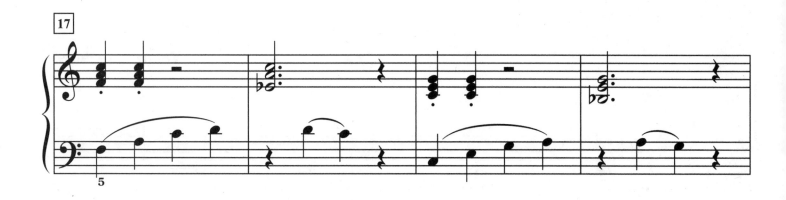

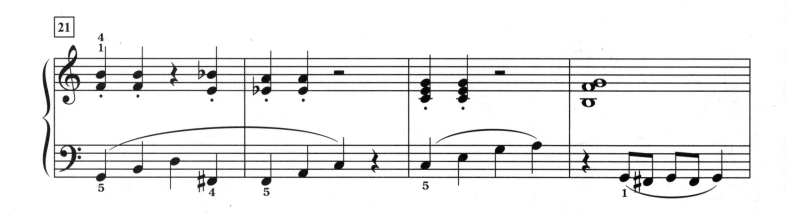

Bird in the Bebop

Saxophone-player Charlie Parker (also known as "Yardbird" or "Bird") was at the forefront of the bebop revolution. Faster tempos, improvisation, and complex harmonies spread like wildfire, and "hot jazz" was born.

Rhythm Workshop

Tap rhythm 3x daily.

Wynn-Anne Rossi

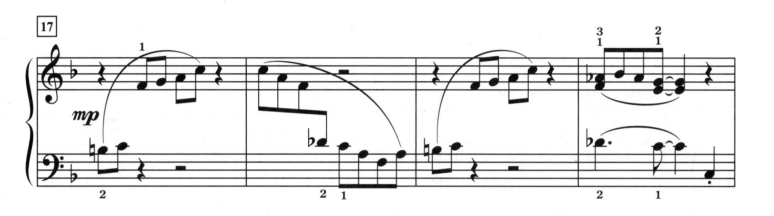

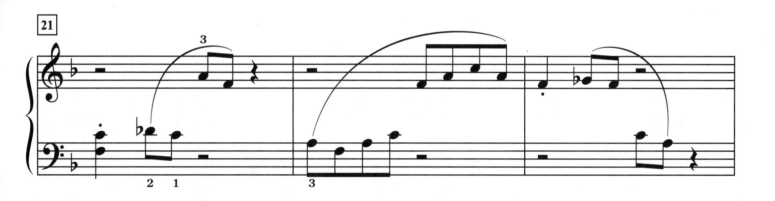

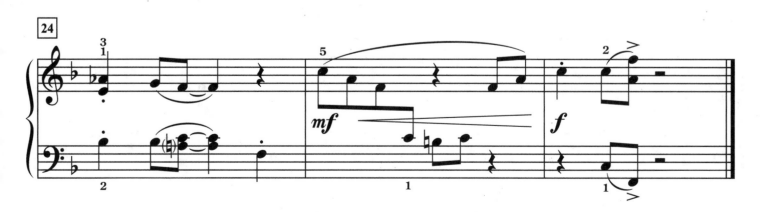

California Cool

A reaction to the complex bebop style was the birth of cool jazz. This music was "hip" on the west coast where pianist Dave Brubeck helped to introduce this calmer, more relaxed style.

Wynn-Anne Rossi

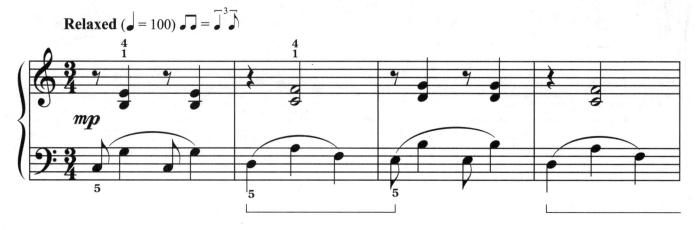

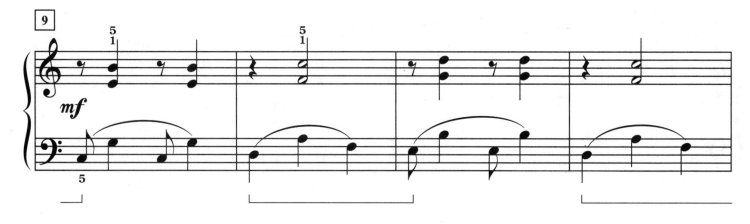

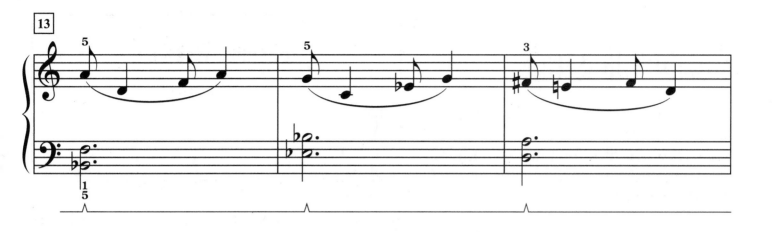

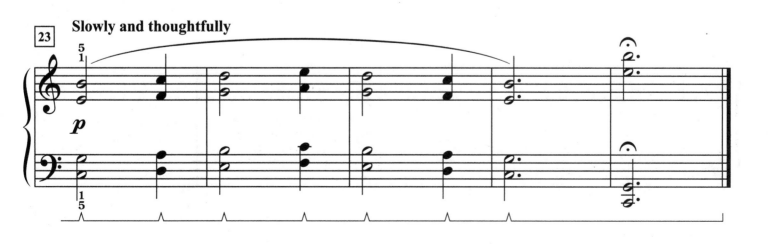

Jazzy Classic

Ahmad Jamal referred to jazz as "American Classical Music." A talented pianist and dedicated educator for over five decades, he has been an inspiring mentor for modern jazz musicians.

Wynn-Anne Rossi

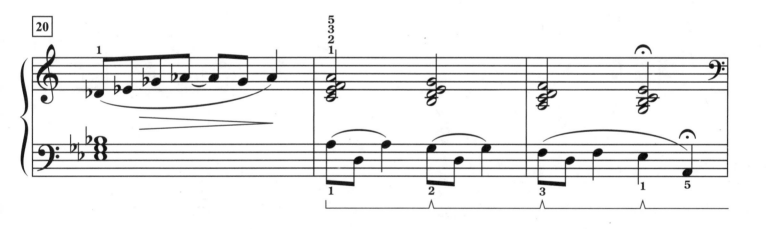

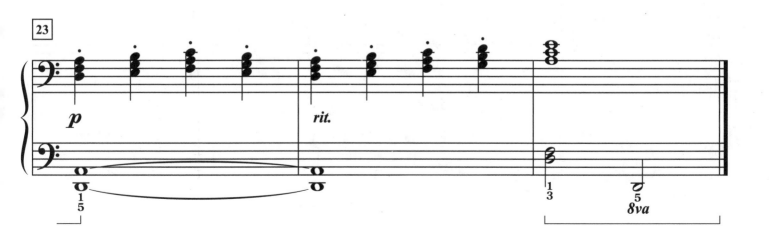

Battle in Carnegie Hall

Battles between jazz bands were social events in the 1930s, attracting huge crowds. In 1939, clarinetist Benny Goodman, known as the "King of Swing," challenged trombonist Glenn Miller to an epic music battle in Carnegie Hall!

Rhythm Workshop

Tap rhythm 3x daily.

Mm. 15–16

Wynn-Anne Rossi

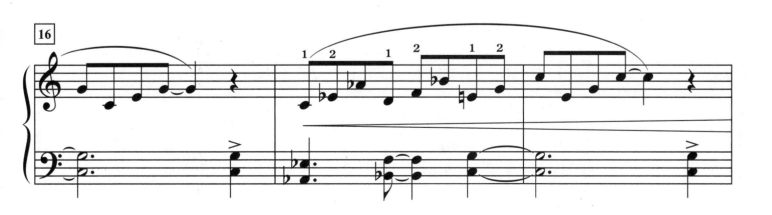

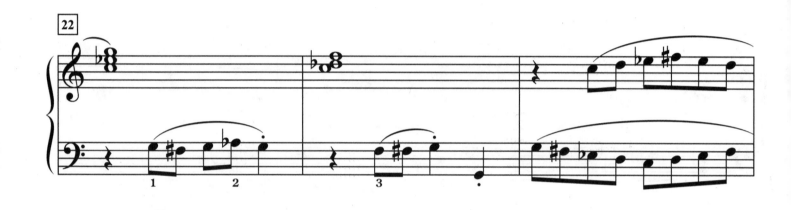

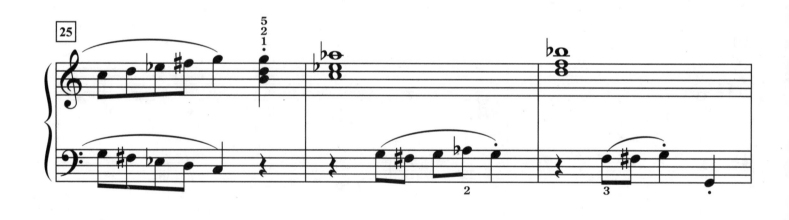

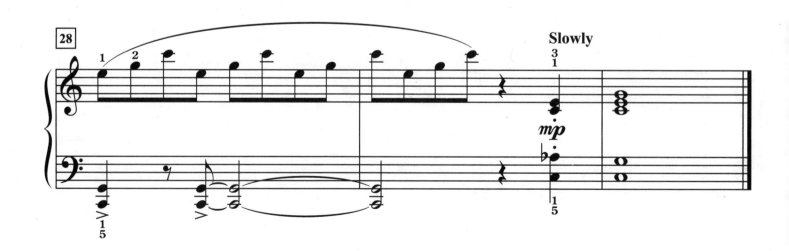

Metamorphic Rock

With roots in boogie and blues, rock 'n roll took the world by storm in the 1950s. The ever-evolving rock style is driven by rhythm, often treating the piano as a percussion instrument!

Rhythm Workshop

Tap rhythm 3x daily.

Mm. 1–2

Wynn-Anne Rossi